Left On The Field To Die

2
Yehudi Weismann

by Ira Rosenstein

Starlight Press

Copyright © 1982 by Ira Rosenstein

All rights reserved. No part of this publication may be reproduced or transmitted in any form/or by any means, except for normal review purposes.

First edition
Printed in the United States of America

Library of Congress Catalog Card Number_____
ISBN 0-9605438-1-3

Truck followed truck off the paved road
Onto the narrower dirt road, and they moved in a line deeper into the forest,
Moving slowly, as if finding their way. It was autumn afternoon
At summer's last warmth, golden light settling on the grain,
But things at dusk in the woods whose light was so scattered and brown.
Children were carried through the shade by the trucks with their parents, sisters, brothers,
Grandparents, cousins — all Jews this time. Trees moved slowly past, sometimes reaching them with branches,
And sometimes the passengers were pushed together when their trucks bounced or leaned around a curve.
Kneeling before him, fingers lovingly on his forehead, then both hands gripping his thin shoulders,
Yehudi Weismann's mother whispered that "We're coming to where the land slopes."

He heard the rest, not yet spoken, and his human sense, eleven years old and
Comforted as late as that afternoon by its infiniteness, burst open. There was no strength in him
As she held him, even as she commanded it with her dark eyes and paining grip,
The forest receding behind her intense face, replaced by ever blacker forest.
He was filled with bitterness at what his parents had done, that they'd brought him here,
Hadn't escaped, trapped him. He had the child's selfishness, of course,
That can rant and wail in the midst of parents' misery, as if the universe
Was all in his own young spot. Then his mind fell deeper, into fear alone. She felt trembling
And wanted to enfold it, engulf him in her warm arms, but she pulled away —
That was useless now: "I want you to jump over the side and run through the woods."

Huge black eyes — her eyes too — stared up at her, and never had he seen her face
So empty of warmth and caring. But continuing to look, he knew she was acting — mother and son
Shared a crippling sensitivity to things. He touched her face. "Don't worry," he tried. She slapped,
Softly slapped, his hand away. "You'll look for help, look for someone to hide you." Look for help?
Boys pushed him down as girls laughed — who would help him? Even his voice meant nothing
To anyone — perhaps some old men. She held his arms, trying to pass a calming strength to him —
He sensed her fear equaled his, but that she accepted her own death.
He couldn't climb over the side — he knew he couldn't. "You've got to save yourself now."
Yehudi and his mother looked up at his father. His mother rose. Had his father heard?
He looked away and Yehudi thought not — back at the passing trees,

Tugging at his scraggly black beard in seeming bewilderment as Yehudi's mother whispered to him.
Yehudi leaned against the side, felt the truck vibrating through his body—its rattling, lifeless metal.
He couldn't move. He feared everything now, simply because it was part of life—
The twisting line of trucks, the forest, death, night, loneliness, sleep,
The noises they passed, the fluttering of branches, gleaming black puddles flat in the woods,
The sudden yellow headlights, the smell of gas. His father said something to him—he didn't hear. He'd never sing again.
They were coming to the slope, where the roadside slid down into foliage and darkness.
The lead truck was already there, out of sight. His own truck began
To turn the bend. "Now," his mother commanded. He pressed himself flat against the truck, away
From her voice—but he rose, he was lifted up over the side and flung away by his father as he kicked

Trees whipped past him the ground whirling up hands out it slammed him, stopped him,
And shook him as he rolled over and over downward and rose, then, the moment seeming eternal when he stood, just like a swimmer
Entering a pool from above, he dived full-length into the dark growth, disappearing
From anyone's sight. Further down the slope he rose to his feet and ran—above and behind him heard voices
Screaming out their Polish at the forest, cut off by an enraged command in German.
Yehudi knew he must run for his life now, and never return for his parents,
Yet wordlessly he called himself a coward. Trees ran at him, dodging at the last moment.
The invisible moon was up. He hurried down a corridor of trees, smashing the leaves beneath,
And things scattered invisibly but wisely before him, the plants thrashing at left and right.
He splashed through puddles, running rapidly. The woods had always terrified him, yet held, he'd thought,

The secret of the world's music, and he was there as he had dreamed so many times.
Bees! He musn't be stung! Not now! Two branches he couldn't see thrashed his wrists,
One snapped across his leg. His throat grew sour with pain, loud, rapid breathing bringing in searing air,
His heart punching against his chest, but he ran on like a horrified, uncaged young deer.
When he tripped over a log he sprang up and ran, nor was he even aware he'd been shot three times,
Not hit by branches. Finally he began to slow, staggering on. He halted against a tree a moment,
Sucking wide-mouthed for air, then picked up his run in helpless slow motion.
The sun had just begun to set beyond the already-dark forest.
Once he fell to his knees, rising, with effort, against pulling heaviness.
"Please, God," he began, then stopped—he would not call out

To the God who allowed his parents to be taken from him.
All was nearly black. He walked slowly forward — was it? He seemed
To hear footsteps somewhere behind. He remembered his grandfather's tale of the little men
Who did live in the woods. Or was it the Germans? He ran again,
Running through the gray light between towering, darker shapes.
Night noise all around him. Finally he had to stop. He sat down,
Sat in a puddle and rose disgusted that the back of his pants was wet.
He started to walk and hit a tree. In his tiredness and fear he half hoped some spirit of the woods,
Or some being who lived only here, would find him and care for him,
Where he could wait for his parents. Yehudi's mind seemed to circle above him —

He wondered if there was some being to whom God was a child?
He felt the presence of many lives — Yehudi knew he could stay with them —
Some without minds, rooted, still, even now. Wings beat in the leaves.
"An angel." He looked up, saw no angel, saw nothing.
He touched his leg, slid his hands along the warm, slippery cloth,
Felt the ends of his coat sleeves wet with his wrists' blood. He went some steps,
Walking into water, knelt to both knees there, a pond's edge, touched his wet hand
To his cheek, his lips to his palm, sipping at the skin, then splashed water feebly
Over his pants and wrists and coat. He dropped his bloody wrists into the pool. The cooling evening tightened
Around him. He lifted himself, by some tree, which he felt.

He could see nothing. He wished the spirit would bring his grandfather too,
Though his grandfather was "dead" — What did that really mean? —
The old man with the hanging white beard, eyes narrowing
At pages of tiny print and script, folding page over page
And chanting dully while they turned, later falling asleep upon the book
As if it was a pillow, yet always awake before Yehudi, soon tugging him roughly up the hill
To the little synagogue, always seemed annoyed, though the sunlight flowed over the green grass
And silly morning bubbled with birdsong — pulling the boy who *wanted* to go:
Yehudi loved song, his voice a clear and vibrant soprano which flew
The long line of a melody like a sea-skimming bird, or broke it into fervent, glowing chant,

A burning repetitious incantation, striving hypnosis of sound curling at infinity for an answer.
Old men heard him with happiness—one morning, one repeatedly striking his chest
And singing out, another shaking and crying then starting to hop with joy at that voice.
He saw his grandfather's head asleep again on the brown wood table
Where he rested as if God would appear there first, before that table,
And Mordechai must be the first to rise to greet him
When God awoke some sunny dawn. "I am the sun,"
Someone said. Yehudi opened his eyes and saw the lights, which
Faded into blackness. He started to rise—but broke with pain, and fell,
Crying out helplessly, unable to open his eyes, but—

Lying there—the pain drained, as if down into the soil,
And he felt a deep, calling weakness no child should ever feel ease his wounds and he stood up.
He knew he should walk, walk on and never sleep, never grow,
Till he could lie somewhere safely. He fell with a dead splash
Into cold, shallow water. "Now," his mother commanded. His father
Tried to lift him. The pain lessened, as if it too wished to sleep.
He stood on land. He seemed to be in a tower. He looked out over its edge
And saw nothing. How high up he was. And it was so dark.
He stared at the twinkling stars nesting in the trees.
Perhaps there had always been darkness, the rest a dream. He fell

Against a tree, held it as his mother's waist, but her soft apron
Had turned hard, to flakes of bark. He knew now that he
Would die, knew it with wordless understanding. He was
Too high in the sky. He looked down. The boy
Staggered out into a dark meadow. Above, all bright stars glittered for him.
But his mind was gone—in flight. He was many voices,
And they twisted together, a river running into that sky.
So he thought, while the small body which fell in the black grass
Lay insensible, and the mind joined it in its dreamless sleep.

The boy stood in the field, eyes closed, face high to the spring sun
And the warm currents of wind which tossed his gleaming blue-black hair up his brow.
He opened his eyes, amazed even again by the sparkling picture of spring.
The rushing silvery rain had taken the morning, it had ceased. The earth
Was moist with it, black and fresh, it breathed out, sweetened and powerful.
Tilting back his head he watched the clouds against endless deep blue light.
He imagined he was hanging from the sky staring down at
Foamy white islands moving over the sea — he almost reeled backward and fell.
The grass still glistened, as fallen drops held to the green blades.
He was healed, healed as earth after an unbroken sleep beneath the snow after harsh winter is healed,

Vital as the sunlight in a dewdrop, like a strong river after melting eager to flow on.
He saw little birds in bushes fluff the feathers on their chests,
Their bills clacked and their cheeks chirped. One landed and trilled
On a long, still branch. Oh what a song our Earth was pouring out
That morning for Yehudi! "Miserable fuckin' little Jew!" A stocky farmer
Was stepping with broad steps to get at him, fists clenched.
Yehudi wheeled and snapped back, knew what he had done — in his spring revery —
He had let the cow wander off, that's what, toward the neighboring field.
But it hadn't gone far, had it! The husky man lunged at him,
Throwing his fist at the little head to hurt it, even crack it open like an egg,

But missing he stumbled forward off-balance — Yehudi had ducked, and fell
To satisfy the man's rage — then the boy leaped up and ran toward the cow.
"Sir! She's still here!" the man walking, running after, caught him and threw him to the ground,
Gripped and pulled the boy's hair and head back, Yehudi wincing — "Stanislas!" a woman
Shouted in the distance. At the boy's helpless, half-swallowed cry
The man shoved him down face against the earth. Yehudi swallowed dirt and
Gagged, his arms beating pleadingly for breath, but the hand froze him to the spot.
"Stupid Jew! ' Let the cow go!" "Stanislas." — the heavy-set woman had reached them.
The man turned and rose from the gagging, spitting boy and looked at neither,
Like a bull caught between two enemies. She moved around her husband and knelt by

The child on all fours. "Now what did you do?" she asked Yehudi.
"He let the cow go!" "Oh that stupid boy," she replied carefully,
And started to clean the youngster's face with a rag, but in a hard, unsmiling way,
As if cleaning a farm animal. Stanislas grabbed the boy from her and pulled him into the air
Like a weightless kitten—"Get him to work! That's all! Let the little girl work!"
And he laughed—it was funny to call the boy a girl. Yehudi, clothes filthied,
Trying to smile, picked up a stick he'd dropped before and ran to the cow—
Wiping his face as he went—to stand by it its guard and guide.
"Come here, Anna!" Stanislas pulled and released—with that throwing her
In the direction he wanted, toward the farmhouse. "Yehudi! Listen to your master!" she shouted back,

But he knew her kindness. Stanislas walked slowly to the plow.
Hands gripping it tightly he exploded "If the cow ever gets into Kawcynski's field I'll kill you, Jew!"
Why? Not really that the cow might trample Kawcynski's vegetables,
His cabbage—though that would be terrible—but that Stanislas felt impotent rage at many things.
This was the couple who'd saved Yehudi's life, and given him his refuge.
On an autumn night past as she rode along a meadow in silence with her husband
Anna saw someone tumble from the woods and lie still. She shouted and pointed—
But her husband's caution—some kind of trouble?—and superstition—it was a night-thing—
Made him refuse. She stepped down to the road and dared him to follow,
Running into the darkness—he turned the wagon into the field.

She found Yehudi face down in the night-covered, blood-wet grass at the forest's edge,
Bending to him as the wind shook the leaves above her.
Close, she saw a Jew or Gypsy face, and though her heart pounded she said in a quiet voice
She thought it was a Polish boy. Above in the darkness, despite the slight moon, Stanislas couldn't see.
She wrapped Yehudi in her coat, not just to warm him and stanch the wounds but hide him well,
His face disappearing into her coat's folds and between the gentle thickness of her arms.
She lifted the boy into the back of the wagon, as her husband sat in front, reluctant and unhelpful, till,
His wife seated by the stranger, he whipped the horse and yelled—it pulled the wagon to the road
And down it to the wretched farmhouse of Stanislas Jagielski. By the fire's light
Anna undressed, bathed and bandaged the unconscious boy, and though Stanislas had cursed when he saw the face lit

And spat and threatened when he saw the circumcision, she rose to that and silenced him
With the threat to tell the Germans of the pigs Stanislas had hidden from them.
"I don't want any trouble!" he'd shouted earlier, the brawler and quick arguer who slept with other men's wives.
But for now he must accept this unwanted little orphan. Later — he would remember
That his own wife had threatened to betray him. She dressed Yehudi in the clothes of a boy
Who'd died of a fever at twelve, just as she'd kept the clothes of her second son, a soldier lost since 1939.
Yehudi half woke and struggled with her, screaming words without language —
She tried to quiet and warm him with soup but he bit the spoon and spat around the room,
Till Stanislas knocked him unconscious with a blow. The couple stared down fearfully at the boy,
Stanislas and — halfway — she — wishing they'd left him back there, but too late now.

They bound and gagged him and buried him ten feet below the barn in a secret cellar in its corner,
Strewing rubbish about, throwing dirt on a wooden cover and piling a huge mound of potatoes on top.
Anna feared a Nazi search. Stanislas sleeping, she worked through the night,
Scrubbing blood from the floor, then from the wagon, burying blood-stained clothes and, as the sun rose —
So fast! — and Anna was walking back to the house with her shovel as the rooster cried out and cried out,
So tired she could have lain in the dirt and slept pleasantly, she saw the truck in the distance.
She hurried inside, shook her husband awake — "They're here!" — and ran out,
A peasant woman with a stupid smile fresh and happy because she'd just risen from her long, lazy sleep.
She greeted the young German soldiers and their smiling, coldly courteous officer,
Meekly offered them food and milk, and conducted them about the farm,

Actively cursing the little Jew they said might be hiding somewhere.
Stanislas — "He hasn't been well." — sat in the house, a milk-white face
Glancing hopefully at the wall's large crucifix with obscenities under its breath.
The boots of Yehudi's would-be murderers, whose comrades and Polish men
Had killed his parents and all with them in the truck after his escape,
Strode over the boy, Anna smiling and trying to flirt a few from carefulness, but though her brown hair
Curled girlishly from beneath her kerchief she saw she was too thick and old to interest them.
The men — these boys — stabbed bayonets in and out of the hay, hoping to spear a body,
Kicked some potatoes aside, Anna's heart beating wildly and her smile disappearing,
Eyed the cow and horse in their stalls — yet already losing interest,

Thinking ahead to the other farms, or thinking how the Jew would probably
Be found in the woods, maybe dead. The officer shouted his order
And the men began walking back to the truck—but one young soldier lagged
To trail his woman-hungry palm across Anna's buttocks, then smirked and ran off.
She stood there, looking down, her mind on the boy below. Yehudi was moving rapidly
Through a forest that suddenly burst into flame, every leaf screaming,
Yehudi on fire and bleeding as his mother clawed him open, his father beside them,
Wings wide, mouth open but soundless—Yehudi struggled to break free, his head butting the damp, cold wall—
Yet even opening briefly his dream-hallucinating eyes never awoke—
Nor could he yell as his father fell. Yet this terrible visionary world

Was his refuge—awakening in darkness, with no voice, unable to move his legs or arms, he might have gone mad.
That night, after the Nazi search of the neighboring villages had ended,
Anna harnessed the horse and rode eight miles to an old retired doctor
She thought she could half trust, half buy, and brought him to the farm next morning.
There he treated the right wrist's light flesh wound, the shattered left wrist
And the right leg's deep flesh wound, triumphantly displaying the bullet
Recovered with a shaking hand, and happily sipping vodka afterward as Yehudi
Screamed on drunkenly—Stanislas had anesthetized him his own way,
The only way possible, and now gagged him. But the boy who'd run through the forest lived.

    •   •   •

Yehudi healed through winter, a woman's care tenderly beside him and the cause of his strength.
In time he worked the field, passing warm seasons through to the next autumn.
He was left to the couple by the villagers, though they guessed who he was,
And hidden when the Nazis descended on the out-of-the-way little village each season
To take what they wanted. Here Yehudi fed the earth-pecking hens
And their dawn-yoddling rooster, took the cow to and from the field—
"And guard her with your damned life!"—dug potatoes from the earth,
Tended a vegetable garden, chopped wood and raised and carried water from the well
And cleaned the stalls and other needs, all as best he could,
For the first time feeling the hurt in muscle.

Anna had called Stanislas a coward for what he'd done to Yehudi that spring morning,
And now the man all but ignored Yehudi, hating the woman who belittled him.
In the tiny attic where he slept, Yehudi heard Anna cry out that spring,
But could only hide beneath the covers during the vengeful beatings,
And later sing for her when they were alone. Other nights, in quiet,
Yehudi lay awake wondering about his parents, where they could be, what they
Might be thinking, did they miss him as much as he missed them, wasn't his father
Sorry now for all the times he'd yelled at him, how could they find him —
But the thought came again and again that he was alone now No! But yes,
That his parents were dead No! No! he sat bolt upright in the darkness.

Yehudi questioned God, brought his thoughts in bewildered whispers to him,
He to whom Yehudi had prayed with a child's immense strength, and sang to
With his magic voice. Why? — The only question now. To be creation's God,
The Universe-Fountain from which eternal tenderness might flow, and hurt his children so.
That he who could bless the universe from end to end filled it with such pain —
The stinking brute! Yehudi tried to imagine God — and saw a Stanislas
Grown into the sky, moving over the world, wading oceans easily. Or worse:
That God was no force that lived — it was just an idea, man's hope. Yehudi's throat tightened against prayer.
Yet still there were days so boldly beautiful, so defiant of what life is, that Yehudi
Called out with praise as he knew, in ancient melodies or invented new ones,

Anna hearing in amazement her little sparrow-soprano, even Stanislas touched beyond himself.
He had the genius of melody, the boy, the river that suddenly flows,
And, once flowing, it will never cease till its course falls
Or enlarges to the sea. He had a melodic manner that was all his own — slowly,
Slowly, his melodies unfolded and lengthened, like branches reaching endlessly to the sun,
No one would ever imagine greater slow melodies than this boy if life —
Man — would grant him his time. The lines seemed to halt
Then fall deeper, there into a new world released from explanation.
Life and death were there, a full song for each before he understood them —
He needed no experience, like Mozart and Schubert singing children.

His mistress Anna played the flute a little, and wanted to teach it to him.
She was not at all illiterate or unschooled, as her husband was, this merry-faced, bright-eyed woman,
Indeed, she'd lived several years in Bialystok before being returned to the countryside, and had visited Warsaw.
Her husband said no. "Who knows what'll happen?"—that was his argument.
But Yehudi wanted it—he'd heard her just as she'd heard him, and his
Happiness deepened at this new sound—even as he winced—with his perfect pitch
Wincing as she overshot or fell below her proper tones—he knew
What they were even in music he'd never heard. Yet other times, thinking this a pain one might conquer,
Yehudi played his mind to her off-tones, daring himself to their other possibilities—
As if through a crooked portal beyond which an unlikely garden might flourish—he only wondered if.

A few minutes into their first lesson—Stanislas in another village
Visiting a wife—Yehudi suddenly took the flute from her hands and attempted the scale
She'd shown him—C, D, E, F, G, A, B and again, higher, C. He'd seen
What holds and release of finger and breath could free that simple slow line into the air
Like a genie, and now placed his lips to the flute and played peacefully up and down the scale,
And next began his own melodies, tapping at keys to move notes higher or lower
Till song was right, and memorizing each hit. He played Anna's own songs back to her.
He stood in pleasure speaking anew through the glistening tube, his magic freshly colored, burnished and liquid.
She stared at him, her awe the deepest of her life, deeper
Than when her sons were born. There was a nature-force in him,

For sometimes it chooses a human as a singer, and makes all that is about song
Easy for him, except for his way in the world. She grabbed the flute from him.
"That's enough!" Several neighbors said Yehudi had "the evil eye" and "the Devil's eye" and "the face of a crow".
Even Anna felt this fear at times, at his strange silences, his amazing melodies and humming,
His endless memory for some things and his instant forgetting of others,
His joyous ease at the instrument she'd never mastered, yet his often
Incredible clumsiness at simple tasks like buttering bread, the knife
Inexplicably slipping from his hand, clattering and smearing the butter on the table, the boy's eyes glazed.
Sometimes he seemed to know what she was thinking, other times he was like a farm animal.
Once she placed her hand over his mouth as he spoke meaningless sounds at her—

"Shh — you little crazy." She taught him how to read music, then had no more lessons to give.
Hoping they would please him, she showed him her few books of flute exercises and short pieces —
But these bored him with their emptiness or timidity. Still, he used them:
Now he memorized what bright and lovely sound — as all were — went with each dot —
And the length that was given each. He played piano chords on the flute,
Notes rapidly in succession starting from the top or the bottom,
And saw how melody was sometimes a "note tower" fallen in a line.
He tried to hear the whole "tower" at once, and basically did,
And flew his flute in its aching or dancing melody over imaginary "towers"
Row after row — "looking down like a bird" — and, finally, began his life's work:

He wrote down his first "flute songs" and "voice songs". But Stanislas caught him
At the witchwork and tore it up, forbidding more — though still
He didn't know of Yehudi's playing. Yehudi decided to write no more for now,
He could compose in his head, or simply sing out in one line as he had done,
It seemed enough, and he soon lost interest entirely in "note towers",
Thinking them melody's winter, that melody needed nothing but itself.
Yet even so, Yehudi began to move from melodic beauty alone,
Like a groom dancing from his betrothed, and experimented with wild leaps of sound.
He gripped the flute and forced overtones from it, he blew wildly,
Trying to wake the instrument to something else, trying to

Make it as free as his mind. There was a whole world in that tube — Yes there was!
The boy was seeking everything for the man, he was tasting beauty and strangeness
To see if they were close, and when she heard him the contrast
Between stretches of unearthly beauty and crying noise made Anna consider
Madness. Yet sometimes Yehudi simplified to that around him:
The monophonic birds, the crisp leaf-rustling or merry percussive plop of raindrops —
The woods and field and sky held their own secret, that was no secret at all —
That the simple can be great. And one other music came to him then too:
When he kissed Anna good-night he felt so sweet and wanted to hold her longer.
He dreamt of little girls falling like snowflakes and melting on his bed.

He stared into the distance from his place in the field, from their long-haired heads
Down to the wind-dancing hems and white calves, and thought there was
A magic other-race in life. Even the quick-throated, knowing smut—
Some of it true—of grinning, superior boys Yehudi sat with
A few times on a log at the edge of the field couldn't convince him it wasn't so—
Purer, higher, life but beyond life, he'd compose for them above all others—
Surely they'd understand. Meanwhile, Stanislas knew of Yehudi's flute-playing.
Several times, coming home, far from the house he heard music beyond Anna's invention,
Performed beyond her power. He was unfooled by the flute in her hand and her casual air
And the boy's absence from the room when he entered. He said nothing—

But there was a pressure in his chest to explode—he hated her for her lies!
Yet as autumn moved to winter and Stanislas hurried the work of harvest to its close
He felt so tired too. His life was unrewarded, small harvests before eternity,
And he knew it and felt cheated. He had no art, he was dead to nature and cursed its life-long hard work.
He had bowed head in church and home to his god Christ—and believed nothing.
He believed what was there to celebrate that was beautiful while swimming to shore in a landless sea—
The shifting immensity that circled the globe and swallowed men?
He felt his body thickening and tiring with years, and sometimes sharpened with
Unsoothable pain when he bent, when he rose, when he dug a shovel into soil
Or hammered wood with an ax. Those comical old men with the holes in their gums

And runny eyes and pathetic stuttering walks—No! It couldn't be!
What was this that was approaching with winter? Even the women
He slept with seemed winter flesh, part of his passage from nothing
To nothing, his brief incoherent moments of ecstasy a song in snow.
For all of this the man had an explanation: he condemned the day as darkness—
Then resented all that nonetheless shone. The boy's music reached
For possession of him, but Stanislas twisted from the accusation
Of its beauty, its unspoken explanation of life's failure:
That few men seeks the best. So he remained a man like an abandoned sculpture,
Its true form never freed, half sublime and half dead. How deeply

He began to loathe again this Jewish weakling with the girl's music-maker,
And now, alone with him, he told this story: He'd heard that on a rail line
In the woods many miles off peasants had watched long trains passing
Filled with Yehudi's kind. They were taken to camps where they were shot or gassed,
And the smoke from the fires of their bodies rose day and night—it never ceased.
Never ceased—that's what was said. Satisfied, as the small boy sat unnaturally still,
Stanislas decided to save his other story for later—the story of Yehudi's parents—
Which Stanislas and his wife had learned separately from different peasants
Who'd been in the woods that afternoon. Stanislas rose,
And when he went out Yehudi ran up to his niche under the roof

And in that trap sped from wall to wall breathing violently, willfully he smashed his head against a beam
To crush out his senses, falling and slapping the floor wildly until the tears rose
And his voice cried out to revile the injustice of God and for his parents to hear!
Stanislas, having returned, knocked a broom-end up against the floor, smiling.
Autumn ended. Winter returned with its tearing wind, white earth.
Stanislas, Anna and Yehudi sat locked in their house-hut
For days on end. Staring into the fire, Yehudi was silent, unsinging—
He had deadened himself. One thought came of music—how stupid it was to everything.
Singing instead of talking! Making sounds and noises. Anna tried,
With her painful need for him, to reach him—doubling the price

Of his isolation, but for now he was unreachable, winter within without.
Beside them, Stanislas drank, soaring no higher than self-pity.
He roared out of control, screaming desperate stupor's own tale
In quarter-words, hurling wild soliloquies of helplessness
To four appalled ears, yet pouring still more hot liquor down his throat,
Then sometimes grabbing the woman or boy and beating them,
His hand striking in helpless cruelty. Yehudi felt as if he was living in a fire.
And Anna was withering from life, abandoned even by the boy she'd saved.
After her beatings, despite her body's pain, she seemed primarily sad,
And sat passively, as if not caring if she spoke again. Seeing her now, the powerful boy

Rose from his surrender to bring his music to her darkness.
His prelude: first a touch on the hand, then a smile, then a
Brief whispered almost teasing measure of song—and he thought with pleasure
How one day millions would need him in this way and he would answer.
Still, the winter remained unyielding, and it imprisoned
Stanislas with them—Yehudi awaited his chance.
A day came when the first brown streaks lay in the field, the happy earth warming
And muddying itself as spring neared. Stanislas went off for
An afternoon to Kawcynski, his drinking partner, and now
Yehudi took the flute, like Achilles his sword and Odysseus his ship, in little.

He played it, put it down, sang, and played again—together they shared the pleasure.
Stanislas too, returning early because of a stupid drunken argument, heard
Playing his wife was incapable of. He swept his hand to the side—he wasn't fooled. "Oh no!"
He knew one kind of man wanted to come over another. And that was him. Now what was him?
And he felt he should kill it, in there, lurching towards the house,
Where Anna, holding the flute handed her, sat quietly as Stanislas entered.
"Get me the boy!" He saw Anna and Yehudi in slow motion moving from him,
For he'd grabbed an ax—he felt like a god. Raving now, ignoring her words,
The mind-crippled man hurried to Anna—she was in front of the boy.
What she yelled at him he didn't understand. Then she quieted,

And smiled, as she had with the Germans. Stanislas
Was a baby, she reasoned, and she would treat him as such.
She tried to calm him and take the ax, but the drunken man held it angrily.
Anna smiled at the child-man, reaching for the ax, and he swept it into her face,
The blade lodged deep and held, blood squeezing out around it.
Yehudi's sight beheld, beyond his feeling: Anna still stood there, dead.
Stanislas wrenched the ax-head free as she fell, blood pouring now, and Yehudi raced past him
Grabbing a coat, out the open door, slamming it back in his face.
Stanislas smashed at the wood with his ax then slapped the door in rage,
Till awakening enough to simply open it. He ran out after the boy, who'd entered the field.

Stanislas ran swiftly, ax in hand, but the ground lifted to his face,
The ax was torn from him and bounced into white then red snow.
The man rolled over in drunken confusion. A few moments later Yehudi, still running,
Hearing no one behind, glanced back over his shoulder. There Stanislas knelt on one knee,
Unable to rise further, his hands empty. But that man hurled his other ax across the field:
"They lef' you mother! They shot you brother an' nother afa you escape! You hear!?
Anna hear!" and Yehudi heard. He stood motionless. There was the
Farmhouse, the door open, Anna on the floor, Stanislas before it.
Yehudi looked, to where his second mother lay, forever beyond his song's healing.
Then he turned, never to look back. Before him was the world, covered with snow, and he ran on.

In the evening, miles away, he stopped and tried to stop his mind but his mind was racing on and he
Chased it and together they caught his scream — he keened like a tortured young banshee.
He would run on that night to a house in another village and be driven away
By a mother and daughter Yehudi's own age who'd visited Anna.
He would sleep in the forest that night, willing to die, half disgusted to awake,
Cold and stiff, yet finally rising and stepping on, no longer knowing
Where he was. A Nazi convoy drove him from the road.
Enormous dogs chased him from the several farmhouses he approached.
The second morning, unable to walk further, without food or water
But for the snow his mittens fed him, he knelt

In the road. Let what happen then happen. A wagon soon approached,
Yehudi still as it came, and halted. An old, slit-eyed man with a gray cap over his forehead
Tried to curse Yehudi from the road — a husky, blue-eyed Pole sat impassively beside.
Yehudi hurried his story out, in a garbled way, voice shaking, as the old man grabbed his whip.
Then Yehudi had the idea to sing for these men his most beautiful melody,
In a song called "Golden Leaves", and the pure soprano began, but
The first immortal line drew spit and a mocking curse — the old man
Wanted Yehudi *out of the way*! The singer ceased, then lowered his head,
Then he was ready to die, for he could go no further, he must die.

     ·   ·   ·

But Yehudi was saved, by a miracle. The blue-eyed man rose
And spoke in Yiddish: "You'll come with me." He'd escaped
Janowska concentration camp, then fled the charnel's city, but first
Digging up the man-enticing diamonds and equally seductive gold he'd buried "in case"—
A wealthy lawyer in Lvov before its darkening—bought his way north to the shtetl
Of his boyhood but found that village Jew-free and havenless, mother, father, brothers, sisters
And all others swept off like pebbles in a flood.
So he fled south again by the slow wagon and the old driver with his
Well-purchased information that one hick's cousin was hiding a Jew in a cellar
And might take another for the price—this mad red whirlwind world!

All across Poland thousands of Jews were hiding from the sun in cellars, attics,
Barns, closets, even sewers, like rats free only in darkness. Zvi Mendel
Placed his hopes in what the end of his wealth might buy and his deceiving Aryanism
And in whoever may care about and answer prayer. He sat impassively before Yehudi
To save himself, trying for the unsentimentality of the horse between them:
The boy, he knew, took him for a Polish peasant, there let it rest, too bad—
Yet the boy's searing tune threw him to his feet before he could think.
The obvious voice, appalled, told Zvi that he was a fool. But Zvi was content to be one.
Men like to shut that voice up sometimes, to reaffirm that we are indeed the dreaming creatures,
The daring daredevil apes, chance-dwellers and cliff-leapers of the universe,

Who've invented love in its dead void. So they climbed together, those two,
Down into the tiny rectangular pit in the dark cellar of the Zielinskis' house in Lublin,
Where an old man already lay. They heard a weak whisper as the trap-door
Lowered on them and a carpet was slid over them—door slightly ajar and
Carpet askew to admit air—old hands felt the boy's face, then upon the man's,
And a voice that seemed to have forgotten speech struggled to form its greeting—
It thanked them in fragments, and tearfully offered the black trench as their home. Yehudi was panicking.
How could he live in this hole without light? For the rest of his life? It was not possible.
Yet Death with its shaking scythe sat just outside the house—it was certain.
The boy called to his deepest capacity as to a god to see him through,

To make bearable what is not so, and to fill him with the impossible strength to live in darkness.
Light only came when Mr. Zielinski—a gangly, silent man—or his gray-haired wife
Or two muscular sons came down to the basement, then a bulb winked on for them,
And the pit's ceiling-cracks lit—such piercing sunshine! Twice a day the carpet slid free
And the trap-door lifted and food and water were lowered in buckets, and another bucket
Was their toilet, replaced each night by one of the sons—how they hated their task.
Light was rare—Mr. Zielinski had a terrible fear of attracting attention to his basement.
There was no room to stand in that pit—the three could only lie side by side or sit.
Indeed, the old man—Mr. Levin—could no longer stand, nor could he have walked
Had he been freed. He'd been here so long. Yehudi feared he too would lose the ability to stand

And thus he always rose when the trap-door did, if only for a few seconds,
Despite everyone's disapproval, his face lifted to the bulb as once on spring's morning to the sun.
For "privacy" he took the longest journey in the world—a few feet
To sit for hours on the covered vile bucket. There he thought: How lucky
Those who see the sky, who could feel a breeze, who hear the music
Of this world, even a tiny bird's part of it—and he squeezed his eyes shut even harder
And tried to squeeze his present senses out to give room to a dream-flood.
He began to hear music far off, and brought it close, the wordless waves
Of beauty that still lived or might be invented—yet a stink filled the pit:
The two men and boy were two miles from Maidanek, the death camp, and from the tireless crematorium the stench—

How hideous was the heat in that sealed pit, especially on warm days,
The three lying next to each other in underwear sweated onto their skin.
Mr. Levin alone counted each terrible day; Yehudi had lost track, and didn't care—
Let day be night. But that old man still measured out time, and it brought him one evening to prayer:
Yom Kippur eve, the holiest of nights—but Yehudi was silent, even as Mr. Mendel
Joined and chanted. Indeed, how seductive silence seemed to the slight music-maker,
How sweetly Death whispered its promise: Escape. On the Day of Atonement the two voices joined again,
Blessing the hole and the God of the hole, covering their heads with rags so the high
Torah-Commanding Lord might not peer into the darkness and see their skulls uncovered,
Though why an uncovered head should enrage God when the death of his people

Left him unmoved Yehudi didn't understand. Indeed, he thought if God
Lived at all it was in a river deep below, and as men looked up God flowed
Under their feet, a God old and dark, currents moving slowly through the stone—
And the picture ended there. The old man died soon after, lifted from the pit,
On a day thousands of others, sealed in shower chambers, smelled sudden, unexpected gas
And moved and then flowed in wildest panic to the adamant door, before which
They soon lay in a pile; the bodies would be burnt, the gold of their teeth saved.
So, though he still blessed God, Mr. Mendel's mind was easing into madness.
His madness took this form: he was unable to stop talking, though Mr. Zielinski
Warned him he must stop. It was as if the words were pulled out by an endless string—

All he had seen must be told: His separation from his wife, son and daughters,
Their death, piles of human bodies splashed with oil and set alight,
A tiny red-haired girl who screamed from the fire that she was still alive—a bullet had failed—
The emaciated man tossed into lye and eaten alive by the liquid as uniformed men laughed,
The baby boy gripped around his plump feet and smashed against a barb-wired post,
Then smashed again and again again again again, as his mother spread her arms to the sky and wailed for death,
Within her shattered soul ecstatically blessing the bullet that finally came for her, Yehudi
Pushing his hands against his ears and squeezing his eyes shut so tight he
Wanted to see no more but they saw every sight, Mr. Mendel unable to stop,
Till the man who'd prepared his cases well and argued cunningly in court

Cried out he knew the name of the diamond mountain, he roared that name—gibberish syllables
That woke the house at three in the morning, and it was enough—Mr. Zielinski and
His two sons, eager at last, leaped into the pit and smashed out the man's teeth,
Tore his skin with clubs and beat him into deadly silence, then pulled him from the hole.
"He must go somewhere else. Don't you worry, little one—we'll save you. Just be quiet."
Yehudi would be quiet. He would break from this world's hold. Why couldn't
Dream capture a man and lead him out? He eagerly awaited what was
Beyond the faint silliness of light and life, darkness where he might command
Tones of measureless reach—then the sea-like music came, and he was the shore.
But as he let its liquid hands close around his eyes, to his disgust the music

Boomed thunder of artillery and droned like a flock of aircraft—
The boy was feverish, thrashing violently in his trap-like space,
Ill and sickened and at the end of his capacity at last, great as it had been, immensely
As he had longed to live and though that hunger had given him
Wings in the forest, he couldn't go on. Rather, he would join his parents and Anna—
And there they were, as easily as that, three suns. "Go. Go. Never come back. And never tell anyone
What happened here or we'll find you, depend on it. Remember we saved your life!"
Yehudi found himself on a street, gripping some money which he soon dropped,
Standing on a corner in a too-large coat, his eyes burning, blinded by the daylight.
A tank roared past, its long gun lowering, and the Russian soldier high on the turret

Called out: "You little fool! Get off the street!" Yehudi crossed the street—
Wasn't he off the street?—his mind so confused—and when he
Regained consciousness days later he was in a Russian regimental hospital.
One kind of suffering was over for our hero—man's *well-defined* torment called "war".
And now? What now? How? With who? Where? He had dreams—but he didn't
Live in a dream, only the narrow tunnel of the world. He wanted so much
And survival was only his starting point. Yehudi felt he'd answer these questions alone—
But he was wrong. A uniformed man stood before his bed: "Yehudi." Thus in two mornings
He awoke in Paradise: The sheet was clean, the pillow soft and deep, a bird warbled
And sprang from the window sill—Yehudi followed its flight into nothingness—below it street and sidewalk shining.

Was the youngster a dice to roll so wildly down chance's corridor?
Whatever, the man was his Uncle Benjamin, his last living relative in Europe:
The Polish Communist had fled Hitler's invasion with the retreating
Russian Army, spent the war in Russia and was being returned to Poland
With the mission of organizing Polish workers in support of their bright Communist future.
He took his nephew to the abandoned house he'd commandeered and sat by the bed one night
To hear the story we've told—Yehudi changing the Zielinskis' name and location.
(He lived eleven blocks from his saviors—and feared them.)
Yehudi recalled horror with an avalanche-memory pouring down on the past and covering each spot.
But only the boy wept. Uncle Benjamin was Uncle Benjamin still—that wire-rimmed intellect—

The "apostate" hated so fiercely and disowned by his father—Yehudi's hill-insistent grandfather—
A son beardless, lucid, coldly witty, sparely emotional, proud of atheism,
Pragmatically amoral, with the deed to the future. To the boy's natural emotionalism
And taste for the extreme he counterpoised a sort of reason and balance:
"Let us feel rage, yes, but *never* self-pity, Yehudi. Never. I have no interest in mourning what
Can't be undone. By all means let us take our revenge on those deserving it, but deliberately."
Then he swore Stanislas would be punished—but the murderer had fled and vanished after the act.
And Yehudi's parents. The information Yehudi gave led men to dig at the slope,
And there a common grave was found, skeletons—oh, a few strips of flesh too—
Huddled together in the numbers remembered in the truck.

What sort of universe is this where such stunning vitality fled mere bullets,
Leaving soulless bones inert in the soil? the boy asked as he
Sat alone or walked Lublin's streets amid what remained.
The answer was the vitality is transformed but to a form we hate—
That intolerable answer. The boy called memory to his parents as they were
In the full marriage of flesh and laughter, for that is what he was,
And oh how he longed for a music tremendous as life's terrible magic,
Somehow to redeem them. How? It must all be made real now. Yet
His very desire—to speak majestically without words—promised difficulty in the prose-world.
And Uncle Benjamin? He swatted at grief like an impertinent bug.

No one sat *shiva* in Uncle Benjamin's house, nor did young "weepers" or "babies"
Find sympathy there. Benjamin had found a sustaining optimism that rode the tragic
Like a flea upon a stallion. The tragic was another world
And he was deaf to its stupendous music, to deep lament
And odes in love's ecstatic tavern, to the epic hunt song of man on his beauty-chase
Or the intoxicating hymn of the soul that fires, sung when doomed.
But that's such a richly maddening psalm—perhaps a bucket of cold water in the face
Was what Yehudi needed most then, a chilling splash to remind him that he was still young and alive
And should *get on with it*. "And we *will* transform this world," his uncle nodded.
Meanwhile, in Yehudi's smaller world, a flute appeared atop a chest,

And not long after a piano in the parlor—Yehudi not only told Benjamin
About his music, he sang for the functionary—joined a few weeks later
By a music teacher come to hear the boy play and size up what was needed.
This Mr. Tadeus Mirska, able pianist and failed composer, nearly eighty,
Leaned his comically long white hair back against the chair and, elegantly lengthy finger
Probing his sunken cheek, old eyes closed, instructed himself to "smile, yes—
But no more than necessary," and "Remember, please—the brat's suffered."
How he hated "prodigies", thinking especially of one other brat in a sailor-suit.
Most of Yehudi's melodies weren't down on paper—but he never forgot a good one,
And this evening he intended to improvise a long piece using them.

Tadeus was impressed that after only a few weeks the boy could play
The piano even adequately—but he kept that to himself. The concert began.
Yehudi's art was naked as Adam then, unclothed in "learning",
And Mr. Mirska's initial impression was loud chaos, empty banging of the keys.
As it continued the old artist loathed it more—at one point—when Yehudi simply dropped
His fist into a tone cluster—thinking of hitting the earth
From the truck—Tadeus' face was that of a man forced to sip lemon juice.
"He's a madman! The little monster!" was an unexpressed thought—
Brutal fourths, pagan fifths, weird nauseating harmonies sans system,
Without a name yet, Western harmony if it appeared some accident—notes

Torn, smashed out, piled, clustered and flung; and the old man was shivering.
Because above all that stupid hell there there streamed a melody like God's flag.
It fell within chaos and was lost. And then the left hand flung away its babel and both hands
Roared out that melody—slumped in his seat the old man—and then that
Melody too was gone, and the journey continued. It was a journey new to Tadeus:
Melodies that rose like rainbows over battlefields, and reminded him somewhat of Berlioz
In a new world, somewhat of Schubert too, and now of song heard
Passing synagogues where those strange bearded creatures gathered their voices,
Now of lines intoned by monks in the clear silence of their stone homes,
Now of mindless and loveable birdsong, or yelling peasants

Or sullen Gypsy beauties mourning lost love with half-opened eyes
While drunken customers stamped their feet and shook their fists and spilled liquor,
And now of country fiddlers with devilishly speedy fingers leering
At the women they made hop. With "Golden Leaves", Yehudi's tune-in-the-road, his
Forty-minute soliloquy and reminiscence quietly and beautifully ended.
"Very nice" when it was over. "Excellent. A, a really lovely little concert. The, the boy
Has so much to learn, of course — but we musn't judge him by academic standards, no.
All that in time. Of course I'll teach him if you wish. Amazing, some of that, boy.
Of course — some of it I think was . . really, excuse me, not what I normally consider music.
The problems — if you will — young man, are you listening?" — Yehudi nodded, exhausted and elate —

"Were in the harmony and structure. I should not at all touch the melodies.
Well, perhaps some of them wouldn't be permissible in a symphony
Or concerto, really — but quite, yes, quite promising in a way."
As for Uncle Benjamin, he hated anything that smacked of "Old Europe" —
He liked to see it bashed up, even at the keyboard. "I'll keep him out of school a year,"
Benjamin thought. "He should be tutored. I'll say his psychological state requires it."
Tadeus was hired, with a flute tutor and other tutors to follow.
But before the lessons began, Yehudi was made to visit the old man's house.
There a huge phonograph with a flowering horn sat on a table,
Two piles of disks beside it. "Before we begin our lessons tomorrow,

I want you to hear two works." Instructions completed, the first piece
Awaiting but a needle, Mr. Mirska left the room and house.
Yehudi sat admiring the wonderful machine as static issued from the horn, and then —
No! What was this!? In the splendor of an awesome moment the world's walls fell.
And there the other world behind. Tone hammered deep and split the mind,
And Yehudi cried and cringed, it rolled and gathered unleashed
Without respite tidal momentum gathering itself again till the boy rose and danced
Oh that! tension-filled rest, blinding release, and at the end a dare —
"You? Then follow!" The boy sat on in ecstatic agitation, as if the
Whole world was on fire — and he wanted to raise the flames higher. It was Beethoven's Fifth.

It was a long time, and had become dark, before he could place a needle on the second work.
It began more quietly, and Yehudi sensed pain. Only a few
Instruments were playing, but Yehudi knew they would be enough,
Moving through a slow passage that rose from the sadness of a great and betrayed human mind
Flowing back toward a dry shore with the blue beauty it had found.
Beautiful sea, it would roll on and cover the world—but already
It was drawn away, and cursed the tidal forces of this world
In slow pizzicato plucking that cried, while below that a melody mourned
For all that is not, in utter song. The five instruments
Drew from Yehudi a music of his own, in breath and muscle and

Bone, deep in his marrow he felt it pull, he waved his hands
Through the air and leaned with his body and when he fell from the chair
He felt nothing, a cello's slave. Schubert's string quintet.
Long Yehudi sat in the transformed world after the music's end.
When he left the house, there was Mr. Mirska at the gate—
They said nothing to each other. What need? Walking the night streets home
The universe thundered with possibility—in his head. He saw life's glory,
And felt the divinity in man. Yet, that being so—and it *was* so!—
Why, being a god, was that man tilting a bottle to his lips and then jerking
His hand across his mouth and grinning—or those two men arguing—

Or those soldiers walking without expression—hadn't they heard the same music!?
Perhaps long ago in Sinai or Galilee or Arabia men had heard music of such power
And longed to shout knowing of it to the world—but before Yehudi
Could finish that thought, or shout, a rough-looking boy with
A cigarette in his lips said "Hey, you!" and pointed and Yehudi hurried home.
Like a boa constrictor come to prey on him till his very life couldn't breathe,
A thought now tightened its first coil around Yehudi's still-hopeful spirit:
Where was the transformation of man? Dark nature and the hellish had erupted
From him and now man could no longer defend himself except through visible change:
Soul-cleansing mourning and exalted commitment, the alteration of

An old to a new world and a new race — good gardeners in a good garden at last.
Yehudi longed for this, had vaguely expected it when meditating in his darknesses on after-war,
And wanted to be the singer of a humanity worthy of the greatest music.
Now up in sunlight he looked: Where was the transformation of man?
In the peasant woman screaming about vegetables in the market? Was that her mourning?
Those men playing cards with intense faces? That brass band marching by — as if millions weren't dead?
People seemed the same, like actors who'd fled a theater on fire and then,
Its last scarlet embers cooling, mounted the charred stage and resumed their roles.
Uncle Benjamin, to whom he talked of this, assured him it wasn't so, that
This transformation was indeed coming, but that first the "enemies of the people"

Must be "dealt with". Yet Yehudi was dubious — then put all these thoughts aside
And returned to his notebook, penning singing notes that filled him with happiness —
"Am *I* happy?" That seemed wrong too. How dare he feel happiness — at anything?
And he shut the notebook. Once again he thought of how pitifully few Jews
Had emerged from their hiding places or returned from the demonic camps —
Then he thought of his parents and Anna again — but their faces were less distinct.
So he opened his notebook — then guiltily shut it again, but felt annoyed he had to —
And confused. Was he no better than the others? Was there some kind of
Momentum to the ordinary in all men? The door downstairs slammed,
And he heard voices under the floor — the old man had arrived for another lesson.

Now *there* was something to be unhappy about. Yehudi's belated initiation into the Western secrets
Of Harmony and Counterpoint was underway, had been underway for some time now,
The boy straining and kicking against each new "must" and "shall do" and "cannot"
And "before you can *break* the rules" and the hectoring old man
Behind each lecture. This boy was a wild little Cro-Magnon, if you must know,
Who had developed a music of his own and fought in two ways with
This new one — to learn it and not to learn it. As a small shaman he
Was complete, in command of a dream-time music, and struggled with this new kind —
So formally conscious, so amorous of complexity, so plotted and fitted, so ambitious
Yet sometimes so cold. Yehudi would pen or play a beautiful melody and then,

For the first time in his life, his creativity went blank. Things—"classical" things—
Were now supposed to happen to and from the melody—but the melody stood there,
A sullen beauty. It didn't change—why should it?—it was already complete.
Yehudi placed a proper academic harmony below it—he passed the melody
From his right hand to his left—higher, lower, upside down—why?—
Rightside up again—he had the flute repeat the line—the result was dead.
Yehudi hadn't yet learned the metamorphosis of melody, how he'd give it
Birth, growth and death within a larger organism it led on through its being.
He began to wonder if this would be possible in his music—and, worse, if it meant anything more
Than a simpler music of song in hypnotic repetition. No, it meant nothing more—

But such was the music his ambition had chosen.
Tadeus, seeing the boy's discouragement, now praised him for the progress
He had made in such a short time and then added: "Yehudi—listen to me—
I'm an old man—we don't have to lie—I think you have genius."
How Yehudi would feast on those words in years to come.
The young teenager was also personally unhappy. Benjamin had been transferred to Warsaw—
Tadeus was taken with them—and Yehudi placed in school—no hiding place available now.
He was a creature of fun to the other youngsters—with his hurrying walk,
Head down, his stutteringly excited speech, high voice—still!—shortness,
"Girly eyes", sometimes forgetfulness, non-musical clumsiness. He didn't have

A single friend, though he longed for friendship, and also "love"—
Whatever that was exactly—yet two boys, as the others hurriedly gathered round,
Proudly told the tale: they already had *had* "love"—one in the woods, another in a cellar.
Some of the students seemed to find Yehudi more than just funny. He was jostled
In the halls, called a "Yid!", had a lighted match thrown in his face,
And someone left this note on his desk: "Hitlir made a mistak.
He didn't kil you to." Pogroms had broken out all over Poland,
As if it enraged the people there that any of *them* had survived.
Yehudi, vaguely, yet less vaguely as time went by, was also aware
That a new kind of Poland was emerging, one with new masters, not freedom,

And that his uncle was such a little master. It was at this point
Yehudi told Benjamin the truth about Mr. Mendel and the Zielinskis.
But back in Lublin the family indignantly denied everything—and nothing could be proven.
Tadeus' advice was to work harder: "Forget the world is outside." But instead
Yehudi was beginning to think of America. He remembered Anna's incredible stories,
Including the movie she'd seen, of that great land of consistent wealth
And freedom and happiness and dancing—if only the whole world could move there!
Yehudi hesitated to bring the subject up with his uncle, but he needn't have—
Benjamin was already considering the advantages of having others raise Yehudi.
He *did* care about the boy—but the man wasn't material to be a father,

And night as well as day was for his cause. When Yehudi finally touched on it
His uncle had an answer in hand, "if you should prefer such an option."
An American cousin—Jacob Weismann—a married man with three sons—
Had been located in New York City and contacted by Benjamin. A new home and family
Were waiting for Yehudi if he wished. And after a month: "Yes."
So it was the boy stood upon a runway in Warsaw with Benjamin and Tadeus,
Ready to board a plane headed for Stockholm. He embraced the only two people
He cared about, and then that moment too passed, and he looked down
At the thread-like roads and neat little farm patches—a planet seeming at peace.
Over a beach and out into the sea he left his land behind, and

On the freighter to New York he loved the hungriness of that sea up close,
How it slapped the sides and jumped the rails—and, as many times, Yehudi was in awe
Of a mindless power, and wondered how ocean or forest might be stolen for his music.
On a pier in Manhattan the composer's new family was waiting to greet him
And take him to his home in the Bronx. A stocky man in a double-breasted suit
Pulled a cigar from his mouth and flipped it out into the river as Yehudi
Came down the gangplank with his suitcases and flutecase, embraced the boy
And then pumped his hand: "Welcome to America!" With him was his wife,
Three sharply-dressed sons, and two daughters-in-law, the younger stunning—Yehudi lowered his eyes.
The sons were furrier too, law student, and the youngest—unmarried, huge and strapping—

A "pitcher" in the "Giants' organization"—Yehudi wondered if something was lost in the Yiddish translation.
Jacob's wife's perfume dizzied Yehudi as they kissed—above her
Building after building rising—above these super-buildings—Yehudi staring up
Till the younger girl laughed—"like bells," the artist thought—remembering, even at that spot,
His dream to compose a great work for all bells. "I hear you're not bar-mitzvahed yet, Yehudi.
The first thing we'll have to do is get you bar-mitzvahed," Jacob said
As he, his wife, Yehudi and the pitcher rolled north in the first of two Oldsmobiles.
But that was the last thing Yehudi intended to do. "And then we gotta find him a girlfriend,"
Rick added, to his parents' laughter. It would get worse.

       •   •   •

A twenty-six-year-old man awoke, out of work. Sunlight hit the floor,
Shooting through the east and only window of his furnished room, nearly 10:30.
"Today—no—I'll take—no, tomorrow—a shower."—every moment precious,
Every second a potential note?—and wasn't music time, unmarried time
Escaping human touch? The last junky had stopped screaming by now,
And was sprawled in powdery fatigue and weird dream. The last drunk had roared
His dark nonsense at the ceiling and the whore down the hall turned her last trick.
But it would begin all over. "God—I must get away from here.
How could I have fallen so low?" How? He was the greatest outlaw
Of them all, a pennyless singer in the Capital of the Machine.

It was time to get up, yes, but he lay back again, that slight man,
Mop of hair still black, his tiny hand that couldn't expand
At the piano far enough to reach many composers kneading his drawn lids—
What had it been, the dream?—something silly, a grinning dinosaur
Hopping behind him down Broadway, chased him into the shadows, wandering
Through a subway station, no, he had a goal, there, in the tunnel,
At the keyboard, approaching headlights glowing and the crowd racing and
Chasing the elusive unslayable bull as Anna flirted with his murderers,
Or the dream-chorus again then sang him through darkness a long whistling scream—
Yehudi leaped up and stood shaking in the darker room. 3:15 PM.

"No! No more dreams!" And "Why am I so tired anyway?
What do I have to be tired about?" Since being fired from
His last job—that unspeakable mail-clerk's job—
He could sleep late every day, and he hadn't left his room in three days,
As the garbage bag showed. It was time to work, to play the piano in his head—
He had no real one, couldn't afford one, but it didn't matter—
He composed in his mind. Benjamin's gift-flute—"good little friend"—
Lay on a shelf in the case he'd carried to the plane.
He'd lost interest in it, actually—it was just one more player in his orchestra,
And not the best—Yehudi composed for vast forces.

No, a new idea: put the Piano Variations in G aside and return to the Trio.
It seemed . . . Poor Benjamin. His God had turned on him, spotting, through
The fervent show of faith, the sin of "Zionism", and all his protests were in vain.
Not that any were made at the "trial" where he stood drugged, head bowed,
Mumbling "Yes" even when he wasn't spoken to—
Dying in the cell where he was locked. Tadeus had written the truth to Yehudi—
The young man shuddered again at the dark terror of a world.
Tadeus: It was only two years since the old teacher had died,
Writing to Yehudi till a few days before, Yehudi's one lasting friend.
It was after the boy's departure that the best lessons began—

No more harrying over technical matters "which you will learn
If you need them, after all." Instead, Tadeus reminisced and rambled,
Told of how hungry the world is for what an artist can give,
No matter how it insists on its cynicism, the rewards it will return,
And, within the creator, how high the delight
Attainable in fruition, should it come. There were stories, endless,
Of courts and concert halls, of Kings and women daring in love—
Tadeus treating Yehudi like a man now—of Chopin alight below the chandeliers,
Beethoven's undying idealism warming a snowed-in country home in Russia,
Or Liszt dizzying Vienna in 1899 with what his spirit left on paper,

Stories of Busoni and Rachmaninoff, and visits to Dvorak, Grieg and Saint-Saëns,
Trying, trying across an ocean, to make the isolated young man
Realize he was connected through his art to a world.
Now the older man was dead. Rest his bones, rest his voice,
Rest his fingers moving swiftly, restlessly upon black and white keys through a lifetime,
From a boy in a sailor-suit into his final wrinkled costume,
Weeping and laughing over mere sound. "And where is he now?"
Yehudi knew that those he loved were so lost. Yet on Saturdays or Sundays
Walking the streets he heard songs of synagogues or the sustained
Ringing of churches' bells. Mankind was in joyous celebration all over the world—

Why couldn't he share it, why couldn't he believe? And then he turned the question:
How can they believe? Was there a believing Jew left in the world after Auschwitz?
Many, apparently. Nothing that could shake them, nothing that couldn't be assimilated,
Even the betrayal or absence of God. What was this soil men grew in
Where illogical faith flourished so? In unwanted darkness Yehudi wondered at the human flowers
Rooted on the human hill, rewarded with light and warmth. He recalled
The bald, chunky man in the shiny gray suit who took the hand of a pale beauty
Upon whose brow blond Mamie Eisenhower bangs fell, those two leading twin daughters
Down the steps of St. Patrick's Cathedral, little doll-balloons soon to float away
In their one pink one yellow petticoat-puffed dresses. The tall wife's

Cool green eyes fell upon Yehudi a moment, he imagined. "Yes. We have magic. Not you."
Yet within his soul, not denying them, he insisted on his own magic—let it be heard.
He was twenty-six—still virgin—tears in his eyes—no, not for six million dead—
For his loneliness and a prison of silence and poverty—he smacked the pillow—
Smacked it again and then kissed it, its stained pillowcase.
But his Trio was growing impatient with this. Trio no. 5 in E for
Violin, Cello and Piano, Opus 507. Was poor Yehudi depressed?
One day in the ferriswheel cities whirling through the carnival sky
Or underneath the crystal-domes of Mars his brothers and sisters would weep for
The sounds now to appear. Yehudi saw them—mistakenly calling it a fantasy.

Oh how this Trio was pressing! Yehudi flipped pages to the middle of a movement,
The second, where quarter-notes waited inside even black lines. Andante
For three instruments eager to press on and finish the play of the night before.
And now Yehudi was quickening, the world, gray-black, dissolving,
And, like approaching marchers, the slow melodies coming—
At their head one pre-eminent, he would choose it, but,
Yehudi smiled this time, he wouldn't reveal its beauty all at once,
Let it grow from fragments, themselves glowing, flourishing in the organic change
From time to time—he was learning the metamorphosis of melody.
And as it happened the audience sensed what was coming they leaned forward,

Those fragments were fragrant, pregnant with time-to-come—
His audience tensed for completion, completion of themselves as well,
Now fully drawn to, fully surrendering within, a composer's progress—
"Another fantasy?" Yehudi asked, seeing them—his pen stabbing
The paper, leaving notes, he hearing the results
As if on a recording and as the work gathered its need was clear, that melody whole,
And it came for all these instruments went rising on its wave at last in their fullness and with immense happiness
Ending the Andante but no longer Andante Allegro his pen a blur like insects' wings
Sweeping into the final movement without pause as Beethoven moved his Fifth Symphony
Directly from Allegro in c to Allegro in C that most magical of kettledrums passing

From one to the next in Tadeus' room a pizzicato ripple on Yehudi's page and cello thrumming
A new melody leaped high from the violin two brazen lines intwining
Up and down the man was seized rocking with those three daring players
Into the middle of Allegro and all rose to the final melody like flags raised in a storm the
Keys the notebook exploding and then the last strings' lines died beneath ethereal keyboard trills
And the work trilled through to silence. The boy-man's head fell happily upon his notebook
As Mordechai's once rested on the Talmud, a pillow for the pain.
This the holy madness of Yehudi's life, how his time was spent.
Hail art, oh hail art—the arrow in the fog. It was 10:30 and dark.
He had eaten nothing. He was still in his pajamas. Two drunks yelled wildly along.

But let us leave him for a moment and ask why this poignant scene
Had to take place at all, why the only patrons of his scores
Were passing silverfish squirming through the cracks of the suitcases that held his music
To feed on glue. True, he was not yet a full master. If each work's a journey,
Yehudi sometimes rambled, his melodic overabundance leading him down pathways
Lovely to explore but belonging to some other traveller. Additionally, he was too taken
With complexity these days, desperate to succeed, to break through
And crack a smile across the blank-faced world: fugues—marvelous fugues—where a simple
Melody-over-accompaniment would have been more honest, polyphony in which his melody tangled,
Too many requests for super-virtuosity, too many instruments,

Too many demands for ouds and sarrusophones and twelve trumpets
With six bass trumpets which no one had, too many—but he was aware
Of all these faults and correcting them, and had anyone taken the trouble
To perform or even discuss his scores he'd have corrected them earlier—
But some of his scores came back in the mail—the rest were lost.
He knew no one, let alone other musicians, he was a high school dropout
In a profession of advanced degrees, a funny little man with an accent
Who froze with people or sputtered in intensity and left them laughing and shaking their heads—
As if his existence was a joke, not a glory. The two appointments with "big, top musicians"
Which Jacob arranged for him ended in disaster—the disaster of farce—later in tears for Yehudi.

His rhythmic sense was so fine, so free, so intolerant of the stiltedness and lack of dance
Inherent in classical expectations, it was practically non-Western, as Tadeus once said:
"You, you play, you write, like an African, Yehudi!" His scores were full of shifting meters,
Polyrhythms, displaced accents, invitations to improvise, unbarred lines, strange percussive effects,
Endless requests for "accelerando" and "ritardando", or "rallentando" and "allargando",
"Più", "meno", "rubato", "non troppo", "ritenuto"—or he said the same thing in English.
These scores appalled the few who looked at them. And the mix of melodic beauty
With unquestioned modernism made no sense to people—they couldn't understand his all-inclusiveness,
The world-mimicry of the art. But Yehudi became aware of his rhythmic "faults" as well,
And more and more he understood he must separate himself into two musics,

A public music closer to people's expectations and capacities, no limit to its power if written honestly,
And wilder rides for the few who dared. Indeed, within himself, Yehudi felt he had gone too far,
Recalled the strength of his child-time music, when a single line in voice or flute sufficed
To stun or bring tears, and again and again he told himself he needn't fear simplicity,
He should move partway backward and take a child's, thus nature's, power.
Yet in his three or four best scores—this latest Trio was one—
He had virtually overcome the many faults all listed, and even a brute
Should have wept to hold one in his hands. No, we still haven't satisfactorily explained the situation,
Why ugliness or boredom or sterility somehow sounded "right" to those
For whom his beauty-haunted scores seemed somehow "wrong", why certain people shied

From his works as if they were ghosts traveling outside of time, things to be driven
From the city gates that admitted every motley mountebank, why a strange pall
Had settled over the musical world in the 1950's, that made this most adventurous of composers
Seem "old-fashioned" simply because his adventures followed no well-mapped system and dared to travel
Along rivers of great melody, occasionally pushing away into jungles from which they always returned.
Yehudi remembered his first and last music teacher in America, Mr. Shapiro,
Again heard that grating, vehement and cocksure voice—the most Germanic Jew
In the world, carrying forward his played-out cause of Middle European 'messianic seriousness.
The man's round face, tightened by wire-rim glasses, glowed in explanation:
"What is music? That is a set of laws to provide us our means for control

Of all these elements of sound—harmony, rhythm, melody—to create art.
Now, what is this, art? Art is formal structure, Yehudi; a balance
Which is always rational. Now—and what is our specific art of music?
It is an act of such control capable of reproduction in sound."
And the perfect means of achieving this control—"to which 'emotion' is irrelevant,
Of course."—had been reached: It was the newly discovered "system"
Of "composing with all twelve tones in a state of equality." Mr. Shapiro
Played the results—chaotic, atomized, appalling—"Does he even know what he's talking about?"
Yehudi asked himself with ill-mannered directness. "Does he hear his results?"
This was a system given to the world by Arnold Schoenberg,

But recently brought to perfection by others, including Mr. Shapiro himself
In various works, many with Greek, Latin, or numerical titles.
The teenager spoke back, pointed out that, nonetheless, tonality unquestionably still existed,
That it was still in use—on Broadway, in jazz, used even by classical composers.
But that was a feeble point, easily rebutted: What Yehudi mentioned
Wasn't music, it was "escapism". "For serious art—no!
Absolutely—NO! NEVER! Popular trash—but it is not for us.
Ours is the way of the future, Yehudi." He thought Yehudi was following,
As did his other student-disciples. Yehudi tried—the man had come
Strongly recommended by a friend of Jacob "who knows about such things—

What do I know?—I like Bing Crosby." And the furrier
Was paying for the lessons—Yehudi hung on. Mr. Shapiro decided
They'd study "something old hat". So one day they listened together
To Schoenberg's *Pierrot Lunaire,* that bawling get of German Expressionism—
And Mr. Shapiro, with a ferociously satisfied smile, said "Listen to it.
That is almost like Puccini." And then: "I swear—it is just like Puccini."
And then, again contradicting himself: "That is the sort of music Puccini was going to write if he lived."
But whether some freshly-bloomed Mimi would have howled so will never be known,
Nor was Mr. Shapiro ever to be listened to again, for Yehudi decided he had had
His last composition lesson, despite Jacob's "Look—I think you're making

A big mistake—this man is very big. In fact, I think you're being an idiot!"
Spiraling into another of the shouting matches that soon drove Yehudi from his latest home.
Mr. Shapiro had ridiculed the boy's faith in inspiration, and the resulting "music with tunes".
But for Yehudi the must was song. Let every tree be hacked to the Earth-desert floor,
His dream remained of roots and trunks and branches swelling with leaves
Worthy of the sun. Yehudi wondered at art without passion, art without childhood—
Wondered at the sight of a whole world moving from its sources into a dark room—
And celebrating the fatal passage as progress. Strange madness on Earth.
Yehudi began to think of Mr. Shapiro's behavior as humanity's natural mode:
Conviction without rightness, a spiritual drunkenness and enflamed stupidity.

Uncle Benjamin had had it, as did the Nazis, as did Arnold Schoenberg,
As did the American politician celebrating his system with its slums and crimes and horrors
As "the best in the world". Yehudi remembered a trip with his grandfather
To see the "Miracle Rabbi" in his Chasidic court, the frenzies that swept his followers
At words which illuminated nothing for Yehudi, sometimes seemed willful paradox for show,
And the feeding frenzy as men lunged and jostled for the spittle-flecked crumbs
That popped from the Rebbe's mouth. There was ecstasy in that room—beyond—lo our world.
In that world Yehudi twisted left and right, looking for a brother, a sister,
A listener, a mate, and found no one. The very human mind seemed unbalanced—
Raving over stubbed toes, indifferent to levelled cities, killed races.

These mad contradictions, the lack of "rightness" in things, drove him wild.
Yehudi wasn't a Richardson who could assimilate all things in a sustaining vision
Of cosmic comedy, but a shocked sailor thrown from the deck by an anarchic wave
And now in the high, dark sea. Some vital connection was snapping in him,
A belief, a hope, that man is great, or God is great, or woman is great,
Or one of these could be to raise his music to celebration.
He passed his thirtieth birthday in deep unhappiness, and many of his feelings were actually those
Of the man he'd considered his universal opposite—Stanislas—
The same desperate bewilderment at how body and the world
Combined to thwart him. Yet his work was oblivious. In despair, Yehudi stared at happy work.

A strange and strong pride grew in him, the pride of a man with hands bled by a mountain.
Piano Sonata no. 8 in a minor, Opus 661. How simple this first theme was.
He gave it to the right hand alone, a single line—it danced so lightly.
At last his left hand—all this in his mind—moved soft pillars of chords
Below it—took them away—added them—took them away—Yehudi was laughing.
So simple. To be untouched, unhurt though every nerve-tip's burnt,
To hold your face proudly above the shining line of tears like the stone behind a waterfall.
"I'll go on like this forever." How relaxed this first movement was,
With its dancing theme and lazy, smiling countertheme, its ease of execution,
Simple lines in octaves, quiet sustained chords. "Music for children."

Yet its "argument" was so tight, fingers locked—Yehudi stared at this latest page
With amazement. It seemed a child-song of new size.
Then he sensed a different—no—not a theme—a figure—stabbing
At what he'd done. So the work would be a test. He felt himself within the music, protagonist—
He would challenge the knifing ostinatos with the new melodies rising in him.
For the first time in his life he felt total freedom as a classical composer,
Felt he could introduce any element and retain control, make total simplicity fascinating,
The totally complex accessible—he barely understood how this could be—yet the correct notes took the page.
This was his first structurally perfect work, in strict sonata form
Without an audible moment of strictness. Even by his standards the

Melodic invention was superb, two or three of his greatest melodies,
Yet unisolated now, part of a larger argument that needed them.
Best of all was the fourth and concluding movement, with
Its great-hearted Schumannesque melody, a Rhenish theme, that tried
To make its way through a modern world of dissonant challenge—
Yet that challenge had a grand power of its own—Yehudi
Was synthesizing, subliming contradictions in this piece that defeated him in life,
Hurt and happiness stabbed each other in strange ecstasy—
The great composer is a crucified god, the sublimely beautiful in pain.
So the structure was clean, the invention memorable, the moments-along thrilling,

The end glowing, triumphantly optimistic—"This is the piece I must show others."
It was a very major work, yet accessible to everyone, he was sure.
He would accept Jacob's invitation to be introduced to that music publisher,
He would rent a piano, practice the piece hard. . . . But the publisher heard it,
Shortly before lunch, and said no, because he didn't understand the beautiful was before him,
And he was a cold, successful man.———Three years passed.
Yehudi sat in his room, locked in double darkness. There
Was a score there, another Trio wanted to exist, no. 10, in no special key,
So restlessly those instruments moved in a song that was wild and unsatisfactory,
Roaring out only dying instantly, chagrined whispers, the piano playing single, low

Notes, or bright tones desperate as a corpse's grin, everything faltering
Particles of an exploded world surrounded by the deep space of silence.
Yehudi flicked the light on, the cello and violin sputtering incessantly,
Unharmonized, without the piano, Yehudi didn't want it anymore,
Didn't want its harmony, didn't believe in its harmony, didn't
Believe in the Civilization behind the harmony or the race that built the Civilization.
Violin and cello continued on alone in slow, lonely lines,
Occasionally moving in fourths and fifths as if in a desperate and bleak
Organum at the end of time, sounding through some emptied church
Where the mice squeaked Bach, all that remained of his Passions.

Suddenly, the two instruments tried to rise in a melody, for it was inevitable in Yehudi,
But he broke them, like a father strangling daughters who wouldn't stop singing,
And tore their melody into mutilated bits, crookedly smiling at the act,
His life's first. A few last dots — what notes were left slowed and stilled.
His music had ended — Yehudi was no longer a composer.
And he flipped the score at the window, watching it separate into pages that shook in the air
Till they fluttered to the floor. He stumbled into old clothes. It was 10 at night.
His cheeks were black with stubble, his dark eyes locked in a stare, though at nothing.
There were two rivers squeezing this island between themselves.
It was deep autumn night, colder than the autumn he'd fallen from the truck, and further along.

The world heaved itself up as he left the building, higher and higher, into towers livid with light.
Greater than that light, like a comet's trail in the sky's past, an epic beauty had come and gone—
What Auschwitz had failed to accomplish others in their other systems
Could bring to an end, repeated each time the best arose, till its bones lay still.
Like jackals finishing what a lion had begun. Left on the field to die.
These thoughts were pouring from him now, not music, in fragments, like his last opus.
"It's all right." The way women have of stripping a man with indifference
To his essence, especially indifference to his obsession, his fevers and frenzies
Though they scale him mountains or compose worlds. "All right — then I'm sorry."
Crossing Sixth Avenue, heading to Seventh — a glowing windowful

Of trash-for-sale caught his eye—"I'll smash those bulbs—
Me." Not fully coherent. Till, after he had conquered worlds
And lain them at her feet to see if her indifference would end,
Or if it was still there, of course it was, the assymetry that splits the world.
"All right." Yet the world boiled with mating—its secret beyond his understanding.
He lunged right—a car screeched around him—a faceless passenger yelling a curse before he disappeared forever—
In a momentary flash a slit-eyed man halted his wagon on a country road,
His old fingers tightening around a whip, how different this world was,
The same, now they moved faster, sustained horns and lights in the night
Instead of surrendering in silence to a forest darkness, roaming beyond midnight boundaries,

Hunting floor by floor, coveting the empty sky from the roof.
Earth was aching in every nerve and vessel and blood-drop of him,
But Yehudi tightened his throat against a cry, and wondered why he'd jumped away,
Not let the machine slam him down. "Am I really going to the river?"
He didn't understand that. Was it for this that he had survived the tree-threading bullets,
And held beauty in his hands like grain, seated his senses before the rising Atlantic,
Listening for its incoherent but profound music, hearing a voice within it—
"Learn me."—how gloriously to try—to crash the very code of the world—music—
Then came hundreds of instruments, their songs, a good-night kiss so sweet,
Cruel knocking on the floor by a broom, darkness in the pit, sudden shots, "Hey, you!",

Marchers loud, men and women dimly on and off the stage, a stench—
He walked down Eighth Avenue, remembered summer conga players, drunken men in undershirts, yelling children
All oblivious to him, to the world-code, "Or perhaps *they* . . ."
And simply he hated life, hated being alive anymore,
Didn't wish to be alive, felt prodigal nature had had a crazy fling
But it should end now, it was too cruel to ask him to carry it forward.
Suddenly, Yehudi halted. He wasn't far from the river. Now—it was time to turn around.
This walk would clear his head. Tomorrow he must look for work.
A clerk. A messenger. Maybe go to college. Be a teacher. Get married.
Buy a big car. Why not? He needed a good night's sleep—"like the others".

But still he walked west. He broke into a run across the deserted lane of Ninth Avenue,
Down Fifteenth Street. "Must." To get away — felt he was being stalked —
That a thing which had missed him before, as millions fell around him,
Had caught up again — or perhaps it had let this special one survive
As a toy in a cruel plot, saving more amusement for later.
No, nonsense! Why was he running? Across the road the giant pier-fronts blocked him from the water,
He would run south till he found it, he would **run** to where the island
Ended and add a step, and his music? he wished to shred it fling it to the burning stars,
Let it return. He crossed Gansevoort Street — and there was the Hudson, lying in the moonlight.
He was so tired too. For a little moment, desired to sit, to lie there, to watch the flood

That would cover him resting peacefully, patiently. No — was this possible?
Was Yehudi really going to leap out into the Hudson River?
Indeed. But instead we show a miracle in the night, in the land
He condemned and fled, the concert on the other side of silence.
A woman was walking her dachshund, it had run on ahead and taken her too far,
And now she held it by the leash and meant to return to a better-lit block.
Her name was Greta Long, an artist, a painter and sculptor and poet,
And she stood still, as the scared dog yapped. That little man she'd watched cross the street —
He lay in the gutter and cried out. She should have fled the nut —
Manhattan was full of them, wasn't it? — but she was a nut too, she smiled,

And daring as a pirate, a man conquerer on land and sea,
Their hater and lover without fear, never, who kept asking life: Haven't you more?
How Greta *loathed* caution, and hoped to die young, or not too old, a joint in one hand
And a paint brush in the other, leaping off a cliff with some last lover
Clinging to that long red witch hair. She knelt by the world's master of music,
The supreme singer of his race, and, just as, weeping, he started to rise,
Touched — Yehudi had not felt a touch in years — his head.
Where the vision swirled. "If you're rehearsing a play, mm, you're very convincing,"
She said in her throaty contralto — and only now was Yehudi fully aware that
Someone was beside him. He needed her. Even God, they say, needed a woman to be born.

"If this is for real, may I help you?", her voice sultry and amused,
Pulling him back, to the world where amusement can cure.
I have to tell you she took Yehudi to her apartment that night,
Over on Twelfth Street off Greenwich Street, a bit down the short block,
And fed his throat warm herbal tea, washing down a crunchy oatmeal cookie,
Joking meanwhile, being even kinder than she'd intended to be,
Because it was more pleasurable than she'd expected—"Why don't I play saint for a night?"
So she asked him if he'd like to shave the stubble off, offering him the razor
Of the last lover who'd fled overwhelmed, and he nodded and she found him in the bathroom
With twin nicks on his chin, and she tapped them one two, kissed the bloody spots

And powdered them white and in the beginning for the hell of it
She kissed him again and allowed his hands upon "my well-worn waist,"
And beyond that trusted the warmth of her intuition into unexpected passion,
Never denying her body but puzzled at what it was asking of her,
Soon far beyond puzzlement or questioning she was in bed with him,
Stroking his penis to rise, and held his shoulders and brought him to herself—"All right."
There Yehudi happily went, caught in the tight warmth that melted around him,
No tightness at all, anywhere. Life sighed, and eased, the chaos unworked,
And next morning at the piano he offered himself to her in another song,
With renewed human force he thanked her, and in the eloquence of that morning power stunned her—

She took him to bed again, his penis ready this time, he was learning,
And would learn more, the repetition of a melody infinitely ornamental and enchanting.
How Yehudi greeted the *next* morning—she was still beside him.
So he changed, into that love of a woman, and through the woman into life.
We view things from different perspectives, it seems, and the music abandoned
Was called for, happily returned. As for Greta, she was forty-seven and,
Though her days with Yehudi warmed her, she thought ahead and hoped
He could find a woman his own age to give him the marriage and child he so desperately wanted—
For reasons she didn't quite understand—the first was unessential, the second an encumbrance—
So she thought. Yet she became pregnant that first night,

A child was put in her, and asked Greta to accept it as an amusing destiny,
To try out marriage and motherhood with her unlikely yet marvelous mate—
Greta knew she couldn't, that this still wasn't for her, and with regret
She decided . . . but she couldn't do that either. In nine months' time, to Yehudi's cosmic bewilderment
And Greta's surprise of happiness after the birthpain had ended, a daughter was born—Anna.
A circle wide open closed with a silent snap—giddy Yehudi within.
So upside down through the black hole and out the white he sped,
Out of his soul's deepest night to thoroughly unexpected dawn, there safe.
Now sing, poem and poet, of triumphant artistry astounding the formerly somewhat reluctant humanity,
And the great world transformed through the small.

Greta had the contacts to put genius to work—and this latest Trio was soon played in public,
Not as we had left it, but completed by a life-quickened pen.
The third movement was swift and torrential, a soul leaping into an avalanche
To shape its fall—and this avalanche fell but as a prelude: to
The whistling of flutes, cymbal-crash, bassoon-laugh, the enormous proclamation of massed trombones,
Fish leaping, birds-a-trill, violins screaming in ecstasy, oboes clucking,
Drums thundering, horns soaring, triangles tinkling, organs roaring—
All rushing to their appointed destinies in his work.
Yes, he turned out to be the great composer he thought he'd be,
And, after a bit of ritualized resistance to make the experience complete,

Like a garbage can at a palace gate, all people treated him very well indeed.
And he treated them so well in return. He met Leonard Bernstein through Greta,
And among the works he showed him was an older Symphony, Symphony no. 6,
For Orchestra, Chorus, Female Chorus, Children's Chorus and Marching Band
And Singers. It was impossible—and Mr. Bernstein loved the idea of it—
Told Yehudi he was crazed and wonderful and Mahleresque, but it was impossible—
So down the aisle Yehudi marched at the Symphony's end,
A child's hand in each of his, other small boys and girls holding single bells
Tapping them as the great bells rang, flag-carriers by his side,
A Jingling Johny shaking its bells in his trail, and then the Marching Band,

A laughing Greta holding Anna on her lap in the hall, the baby happy,
The orchestra answering oceanically, Bernstein almost thrown by ecstasy from the podium,
The children singing as Yehudi mounted the stage, climbing beyond the Chorus,
Then above the Female Chorus, and over the Children's Chorus,
Climbed to the Symphony's finale, joining his tenor to the younger sopranos and others,
His song realized at last, the hundreds of instruments and hundreds of voices
Rising higher and higher, Yehudi looking out through his tears
At the thousands leaping to their feet—yet his music had only begun.
Score after score marched out, his mastery growing monstrous, unto three-hour Symphonies
Knit tight as sea-knots, gripping from their first gesture to the final instant,

His one-movement two-hour Symphony moving in a single arc from *pppp* to solar-hurricane and back,
Tone poems—*Ygdrasil*—myth—*The City*—man—*A Thrush Song*—
Every music his, primal and modern, movie scores, musicals, jazz,
Rock, experiments in raga, concertos and sonatas for every virtuoso of every shape and instrument,
And the simplest happy pieces for amateurs at home—he did not forget them—
Drawing men further into the community of music, away from their madness.
Stupid, pinched ugliness and sterility fell before his unquestioned onslaught,
And the great music returned again, first through Yehudi, then in those he gave courage to,
The new Mozarts and Schuberts who had always been there but been afraid,
And finally in the Twenty-First Century Yehudi modestly extended his hand

To the new super-Mozart he made possible, a further expansion of human possibility.
And as this renewed art flooded upon the often-ugly world some men asked
Why ugliness of their own should nonetheless continue, why beauty should be limited to sound.
From this second seed a second restoration was born,
And upon this ever-renewed world Yehudi sustained his powers and even grew,
Until his harp-sound went rippling like plangent laughter through the closing measures of his final Symphony
Through the trees above where his prostrate body lay in a moon's chill light,
And no Anna ran into the field for him. No, but he was found by others,
Roughness in their hands, and eventually brought behind barbed wire, his voice caged,
And one day he stood at the edge of a pit where gassed or shot bodies burned,

And a voice called out "You! There is a body for you to carry!"
Yehudi ran for the body but there was no body, and he looked
Into the face of the man with the pistol, and the man was grinning:
"*Ja*. You. Come." Yehudi saw across the little stretch
Of brown earth, the billowing gray smoke ahead, the low wooden
Humanity-packed buildings behind him—"*Ja*. You. Come!"
And then there was nothing to do but walk, as he did,
With dignity and strange unconcern, a weariness willing to surrender life,
An ecstasy that didn't need it anymore, a music that didn't need sound,
Never needed to be written or heard—it was enough—he had held it within.

"So this is how I die." The man with the pistol
Was making a show of dangling a cigarette from his lips—
Human beings like to do such things—and made an obscene gesture—
As if that could touch Yehudi now. Yehudi walked on,
And when he passed the man and stood at the lip of the pit
He knew a gun was being raised behind his back—
The crystal of Earth-light to shatter forever.
But in some other life, in an alternative to our world,
When he spread his arms the multitudes below him lived,
They did not burn, they rose and sang, his voice with theirs,

Lifting them higher, into the heaven of his music,

Spread wider and wider, his arms in welcome, never to close.